# PAPER PLANES

ARCTURUS

**ARCTURUS**

This edition published in 2015 by Arcturus Publishing Limited
26/27 Bickels Yard, 151–153 Bermondsey Street,
London SE1 3HA

ISBN: 978-1-78599-191-2
CH004974NT
Supplier 13, Date 1015, Print Run 4674

Models and photography: Michael Wiles and Belinda Webster
Text: Jenni Hairsine
Design: Grant Kempster and Tokiko Morishima
Edited: Annabel Stones, Samantha Noonan & Joe Fullman

Printed in China

# Contents

# Welcome

...to the high-flying world of making paper planes!

In this book, you will discover how to create the most incredible aircraft. From sleek jets to jumbo gliders, you can have a huge fleet of your own, all made from paper!

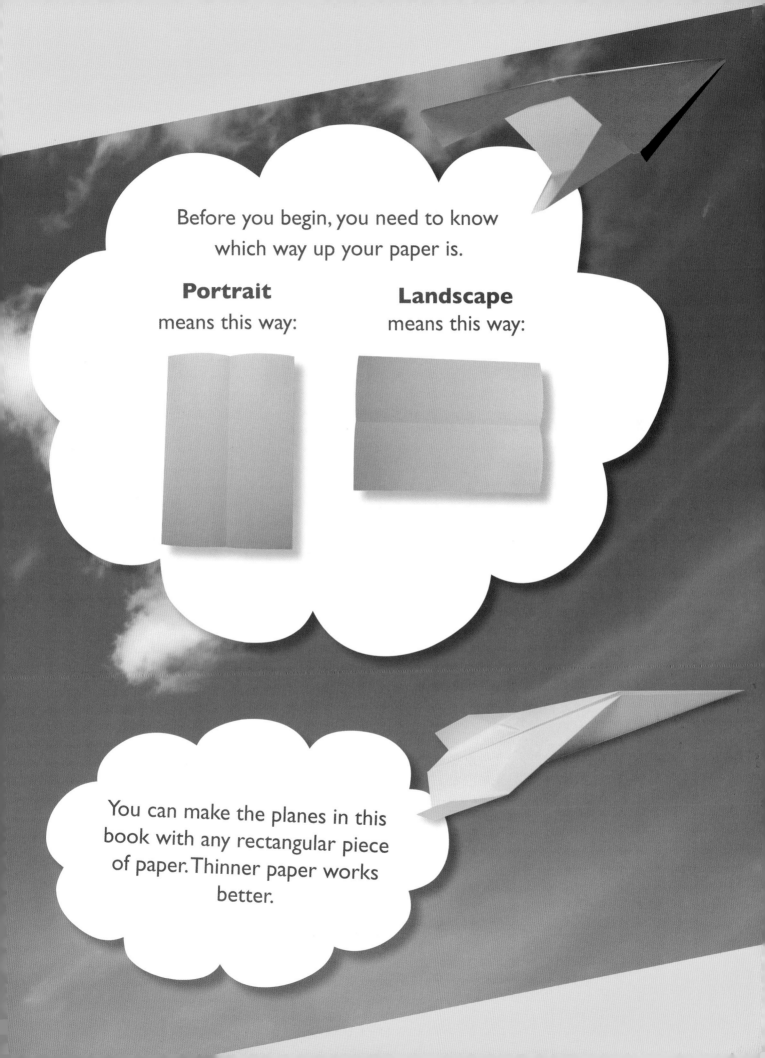

Before you begin, you need to know which way up your paper is.

**Portrait**
means this way:

**Landscape**
means this way:

You can make the planes in this book with any rectangular piece of paper. Thinner paper works better.

# The Classic

A classic jet with added aerodynamic features.

**1** Place your paper so that it is portrait. Fold it from left to right down the middle line, then unfold it again.

**2** Fold the left-hand corner into the middle, making sure to line up the top edge with the middle crease.

**3** Repeat step 2 on the right-hand corner.

**4** Fold the top left-hand diagonal side into the middle crease.

**5** Repeat this step for the right-hand diagonal side.

**6** Fold the left side over to the right, using the middle fold you made in step 1.

**7** Lift the top flap and fold it over to the left. It should overlap the straight edge a little bit, as shown. This forms the first wing.

**8** Turn your plane over and repeat step 7 to form the second wing. Make sure the wings are the same size.

**9** Now fold back the top wing a little to create a wing tip.

**10** Turn over your plane and repeat step 9 for the second wing, making sure the folded edges align with each other.

**11** Holding the plane by the long middle fold, open out the wings, and adjust the wing tips. Now you're ready to fly!

# Dashing Dart

An aerodynamic flat plane
with piercing performance.

**1** Place your paper so that it is landscape and fold it down the middle from left to right. Now unfold it again.

**2** Fold the left-hand edge into the middle, lining up the left edge with the central crease.

**3** Repeat step 2 on the right-hand side of the paper, so that the two outside edges now meet at the middle crease.

**4** Now fold down the top left-hand edge so that it aligns with the middle crease.

**5** Repeat step 4 on the top right-hand edge, so that a point is formed at the top.

**6** Fold the top left-hand diagonal edge into the middle, aligning with the middle crease.

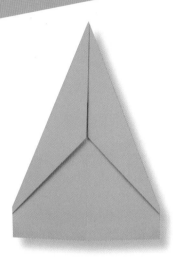

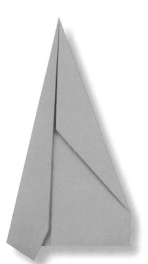

**7** Repeat step 6 on the top right-hand diagonal edge.

**8** Now fold the new left-hand diagonal edge into the middle, again aligning with the middle crease.

**9** Repeat step 8 on the right-hand side. You will need to press more firmly as the folds make the paper more resistant.

**10** Turn the paper over so that the wings are underneath.

**11** Fold the right-hand side over to the left, using the middle fold you made in step 1. Make sure that the edges align and are not overlapping.

**12** Holding all the central folds together, open out the wings to form a flat surface on top of the plane. Your dart is ready to dash through the sky!

# The Javelin

The Javelin is the perfect paper plane to fly long distances.

**1** Place your paper so that it is portrait. Fold it from left to right down the middle line, then unfold it again.

**2** Fold the left-hand edge of the paper into the central crease.

**3** Repeat step 2 with the right-hand edge of the paper, making sure both edges align along the central crease.

**4** Fold the top left-hand corner down so that it aligns with the central crease.

**5** Repeat step 4 on the right-hand corner. You will have a triangle shape at the top of your paper.

**6** Fold the top left-hand diagonal edge inwards to align with the central crease.

**7** Repeat step 6 on the right-hand diagonal edge, making sure both edges align at the central crease.

**8** Turn your paper over and fold it in half, from right to left, using the central crease you made in step 1.

## 9

Lift up the right-hand corner of the top flap and fold it diagonally from just below the nose almost to the bottom left-hand corner.

## 10

Turn your plane over and repeat step 9 on the left-hand corner.

## 11

Take the bottom flap and fold it up in the same way as you did in steps 9 and 10. Now, unfold it.

## 12

Turn the plane over and repeat step 11 on the other side, using the crease you just made.

## 13

Open out your plane, as shown. You will see a 'W' shape. From underneath, push the bottom part of the middle crease upward and pinch it together.

**14** Press the plane together, so the tail fin is pointing upward inside, and press down on all the folds.

**15** Now fold the top point downward so it aligns with the back of the plane.

**16** Turn the plane over and do the same on the other side.

**17** You open out the nose and tail flaps and your brilliant Javelin is ready to fly!

13

# Upside Down

Turn everything on its head with this craftily canny upside-down glider!

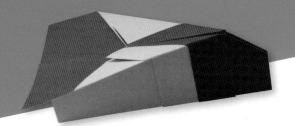

**1** Place your paper so that it is portrait. Fold it from left to right down the middle line, then unfold it again.

**2** Now fold the paper in half again but horizontally from top to bottom.

**3** Fold the top flap upward to meet the top edge.

**4** Now fold the new top edge downward halfway, as shown. Your paper should now have three sections (or stripes) across its top half.

**5** Turn your paper over and fold the bottom edge up to meet the top edge. Make a crease and unfold to reveal a cross where the two folds meet at the central point.

**6** Now fold the top right-hand corner diagonally towards the middle point, where the cross is.

14

**7** Repeat step 6 on the top left-hand corner, making sure the two corners meet at the middle cross point.

**8** Fold your paper vertically in half from right to left.

**9** Now fold the top flap from left to right so that is parallel with the straight edge. This creates a wing.

**10** Turn the plane over and repeat step 9 on the other side to create the second wing. Press firmly to create strong creases.

**11** Open out the wings and you'll see the stripes across the top. Ready, steady, throw!

# Pocket Glider

Air pockets are aplenty with this super-flying Pocket Glider.

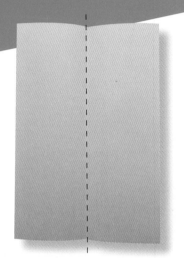

**1** Place your paper so that it is portrait. Fold it from left to right down the middle line, then unfold it again.

**2** Now fold the paper in half from top to bottom, then unfold it. You have created a central cross where the creases meet.

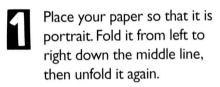

**3** Fold the top edge of the paper downward so the edge meets the central crease line that you created in step 2.

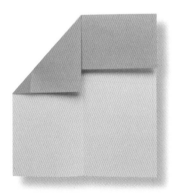

**4** Now fold the top left-hand corner into the middle crease, making sure the edge aligns with if perfectly.

**5** Repeat step 4 on the right-hand corner. Both corners should align along the middle crease.

**6** Fold the top point downward, stopping a short way from the bottom edge, as shown.

**7** Now fold the bottom point upward to align with the top straight edge of the paper. The point should fall directly in the middle crease.

**8** Carefully fold in the top left-hand corner so that the top edge of your paper aligns with the middle crease. Unfold this.

**9** Now, make another fold inwards so that the top edge of your paper aligns with the fold you created in step 8. Unfold this.

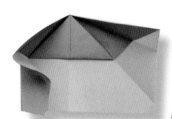

**10** Repeat steps 8 and 9 on the top right-hand corner.

**11** Finally, fold the top left-hand corner again but this time push the corner under the central pocket that has formed. It helps to pull this pocket outwards while you press the corner under. The remaining paper should fall diagonally from the middle of the pocket out towards the wing edge.

**12** Repeat step 11 on the right-hand corner, then turn the plane over.

**13** Press all your creases firmly and launch your glider by holding on to the pocket!

# The Condor

This glider can swoop low and smoothly, just like a real condor!

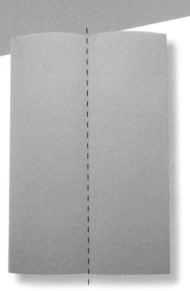

**1** Place your paper so that it is portrait. Fold it from left to right down the middle line, then unfold it again.

**2** Now fold the paper in half again, but this time horizontally from top to bottom. Unfold again.

**3** Fold down the top edge so it aligns with the horizontal middle crease.

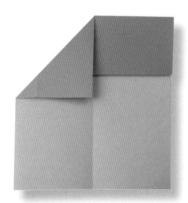

**4** Fold the top left-hand corner inwards so that the top edge aligns with the middle crease.

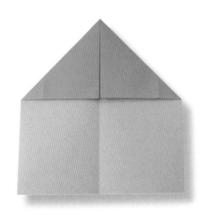

**5** Repeat step 4 on the right-hand corner. Both corners should align along the central crease.

**6** Fold the top point downward using the fold you made in step 2 as your fold line.

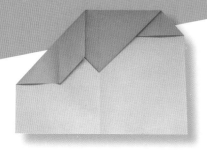

**7** Now fold the top left corner inwards. It should run parallel to the middle crease, but be a short distance away, as shown.

**8** Repeat step 7 on the top right corner. You will need to press the creases firmly as the paper becomes thicker.

**9** Fold the plane in half vertically along the middle fold from left to right, using the fold you made in step 1.

**10** Fold the top flap back over to the left to create the first wing. The fold should naturally sit where your fold from step 7 was made.

**11** Now fold back the left edge a short way to create the wing tip, as shown.

**12** Turn the plane over and repeat steps 10 and 11 to create the other wing and wing tip. Make sure your wing tips are the same size as each other.

**13** Holding your plane by its central folds, open out the wings and adjust the wing tips. Now your glider is ready to take to the skies!

# Interceptor

The Interceptor is stealthy and very fast, so it's great for secret flights!

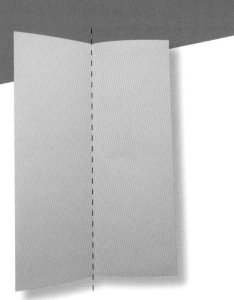

**1** Place your paper so that it is portrait. Fold it from left to right down the middle line, then unfold it again.

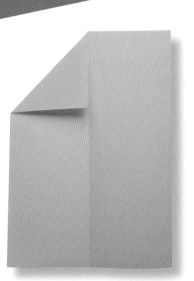

**2** Fold the top left-hand corner down so that the top edge aligns with the middle crease.

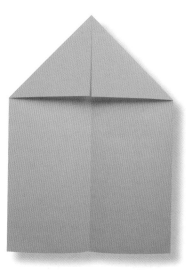

**3** Repeat step 2 for the top right-hand corner.

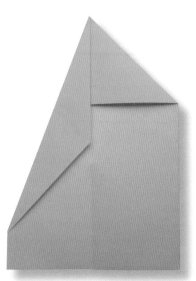

**4** Now fold the left-hand side inwards so that the diagonal edge aligns with the middle crease.

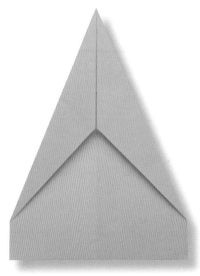

**5** Repeat step 4 for the right-hand side. Make sure the edges align along the middle crease.

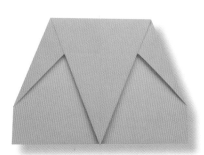

**6** Now fold the paper downward in half, so that the top point touches the bottom edge of the paper.

**7** Fold the point back upward, making a horizontal crease where the triangle meets the diagonal inner edges.

**8** Turn your paper over and fold in half, vertically from right to left.

**9** Now fold the bottom right corner up a little way, as shown.

**10** Turn the paper over and repeat step 9 reversing the fold you just made.

**11** Unfold the plane a little and push the lower triangle inwards. Then refold as before.

**12** With the plane on its side, fold the top flap over to the right to create the first wing. The fold should be parallel to the main body of the plane.

**13** Do the same with the other wing, so it aligns with the first.

**14** Fold the bottom edge of the top wing upward a short way, as shown.

**15** Do the same with the other wing tip, making sure the folds align.

**16** With its menacingly sharp nose and wing tips, your Interceptor is prepared for action!

21

# Barracuda

The Barracuda will cut through the air with its sharp nose!

**1** Place your paper so that it is portrait. Fold it from left to right down the middle line, then unfold it again.

**2** Fold the top left-hand corner down so that the top edge aligns with the middle crease.

**3** Repeat step 2 for the top right-hand corner. Leave these folds in place to create a triangle point at the top of the paper.

**4** Now fold the top of the paper downward diagonally. The right-hand side of the triangle should line up with the right-hand side of the paper. Unfold again.

**5** Repeat step 4 on the other side, aligning the left-hand side of the triangle with the left-hand side of the paper. Unfold again.

**6** Turn the paper over and you will see a cross-shape with the vertical fold running through it. Fold the top downward horizontally, using the middle of the cross as a guide. Unfold again.

**7** Turn the paper back over and you will see that the horizontal fold line lifts towards you. Pinch these together and refold the lower diagonal creases one at a time, beginning with the left. This will cause the paper to fold downward so that the triangle points downward.

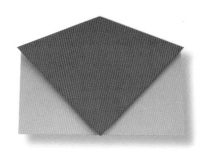

**8** Now fold the point of the triangle back upward, using the beginning of the diagonals as the guide for your horizontal crease.

**9** Fold the left-hand side of the diagonal edge towards the right. Unfold.

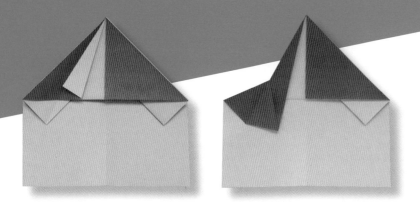

**10** Now fold the left top flap a little way to the left. The edge should align with the crease from step 9. Repeat the fold you made in step 9 over the top of this smaller fold.

**11** Repeat steps 9 and 10 for the right-hand side of the paper. The piece nearest to the middle fold will tuck underneath the bigger piece.

**12** Tuck the bottom left point underneath itself, as shown.

**13** Repeat step 12 on the right-hand side and press both sides down firmly.

**14** Turn your plane over and fold vertically from right to left.

**15** Fold the top flap over to the right, as shown. This creates the first wing.

**16** Turn the plane over and repeat step 15 on the other side. Make sure the wings are symmetrical.

**17** Creating wing tips for this plane is optional. If you want wing tips, fold back a narrow strip along each wing's edge.

**18** Your Barracuda aircraft is ready for its first stealth mission!

# The Kite

Accurate and with massive
wings; it can only be the Kite!

**1** Place your paper so that it
is portrait. Then, fold the top
down, as shown.

**2** Repeat step 1 a total
of eight times, each
time folding the
crease down firmly.

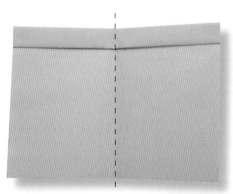

**3** Now fold your paper
in half, vertically from
right to left.

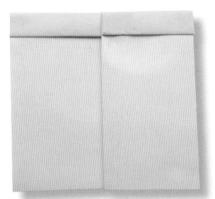

**4** Fold back the right-hand side, making a crease a short way from the middle fold. This will create the first wing.

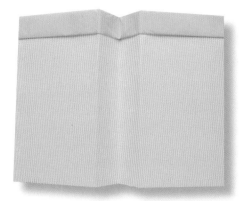

**5** Turn the paper over and repeat step 4 to create the other wing. Make sure your wings align and their folds are symmetrical.

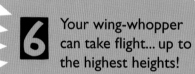

**6** Your wing-whopper can take flight... up to the highest heights!

# Viper Ring

It's all in the throw with this unbelievable paper Viper Ring!

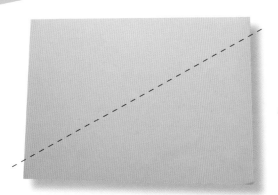

**1** Place your paper so that it is landscape. Then, fold it diagonally, as shown. The fold should be a short way from the corners.

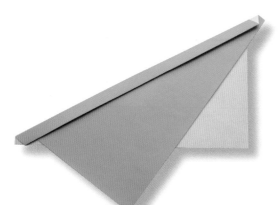

**2** Fold the straight edge (where your first fold is) symmetrically inwards by about a finger width.

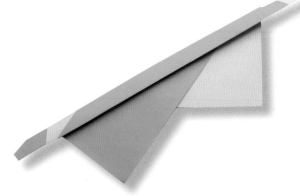

**3** Repeat step 2 three times more to make this edge thicker. You should have four folds along the same long, narrow edge.

**5** Using the folded edge, you will be able to join the two ends by inserting one into the other.

**4** Now you need to carefully but firmly bend your paper round, keeping the long folded edge on the inside.

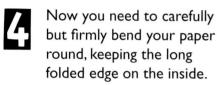

**6** The four folds along the diagonal line will have created pockets at the edges in which you can find room to slot one side into the other to secure the ring shape.

**7** It's a strange one for sure! Throw it safely from a great height and watch it spin!

# The Star

A flick of the wrist will shoot this star through the air!

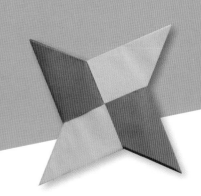

**1** You will need two squares of paper for this Star. Fold the first in half, horizontally from top to bottom, then unfold.

**2** Now fold the top edge downward so the top edge aligns with the horizontal middle crease.

**3** Repeat step 2 with the bottom edge, aligning the bottom edge with the middle crease.

**4** Fold the paper in half, horizontally from top to bottom.

**5** Now fold the paper in half again, this time vertically from left to right. Unfold this crease.

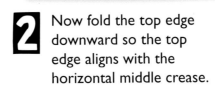

**6** Repeat steps 1 to 5 with the other piece of square paper. Ideally, choose a different shade.

**7** Take your first piece of paper and fold the bottom left-hand corner upward so the left edge aligns with the top edge.

**8** Repeat step 7 with the top right-hand corner, aligning the right edge with the bottom edge.

**9** Take your second piece of paper and fold the top left-hand corner downward so the left edge aligns with the bottom edge.

**10** Repeat step 9 with the bottom right-hand corner, aligning the right edge with the top edge.

**11** Take your first piece of paper and fold the top left edge diagonally to align with the middle crease.

**12**

Repeat step 11 with the bottom right edge. Align the bottom edge with the middle crease.

**13**

Take your second piece of paper and fold the bottom left edge diagonally to align with the middle crease. Repeat with the top right edge.

**14**

Turn the first piece of paper over and place it so the largest strip is vertical. Now place the second piece of paper across the first, horizontally.

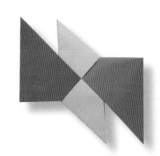

**15** Now fold the top triangle (from the first piece of paper) downward and tuck it into the left triangle (from the second piece of paper.)

**16** Fold the bottom triangle (from the first piece of paper) upward. Tuck it into the right triangle (from the second piece of paper) and press the folds firmly to make sure they are secure.

**17** Carefully turn over the whole paper and fold the top right triangle (from the second piece of paper) diagonally and tuck it into the lower triangle (from the first piece of paper.)

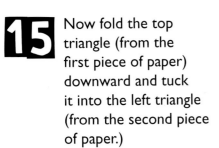

**18** Fold the lower left triangle (from the second piece of paper) diagonally and tuck it into the upper triangle (from the first piece of paper.)

**19** When you've pressed the creases down very firmly your amazing shooting star is ready to throw! Watch it go!